GEARED FOR GROWTH BIBLE STUDIES

SERVING THE LORD

A STUDY OF JOSHUA

BIBLE STUDIES TO IMPACT THE LIVES OF ORDINARY PEOPLE

Christian Focus Publications

The Word Worldwide

Written by Dorothy Russell

Christian Focus Publications

publishes books for all ages

Our mission statement –

STAYING FAITHFUL

In dependence upon God we seek to help make His infallible word, the Bible, relevant. Our aim is to ensure that the Lord Jesus Christ is presented as the only hope to obtain forgiveness of sin, live a useful life and look forward to heaven with Him.

REACHING OUT

Christ's last command requires us to reach out to our world with His gospel. We seek to help fulfill that by publishing books that point people towards Jesus and help them develop a Christ-like maturity. We aim to equip all levels of readers for life, work, ministry and mission.

Books in our adult range are published in three imprints.

Christian Focus contains popular works including biographies, commentaries, basic doctrine, and Christian living. Our children's books are also published in this imprint.

Mentor focuses on books written at a level suitable for Bible College and seminary students, pastors, and other serious readers; the imprint includes commentaries, doctrinal studies, examination of current issues, and church history.

Christian Heritage contains classic writings from the past.

For details of our titles visit us on our website
www.christianfocus.com

ISBN 1-85792-889-X

Copyright © WEC International

Published in 2003 by
Christian Focus Publications, Geanies House,
Fearn, Ross-shire, IV20 1TW, Scotland
and
WEC International, Bulstrode, Oxford Road,
Gerrards Cross, Bucks, SL9 8SZ

Cover design by Alister MacInnes

Printed and bound by J W Arrowsmith, Bristol

CONTENTS

QUESTIONS AND NOTES

ANSWER GUIDE

PREFACE

GEARED FOR GROWTH

'Where there's LIFE there's GROWTH:
Where there's GROWTH there's LIFE.'

WHY GROW a study group?

Because as we study the Bible and share together we can

- learn to combat loneliness, depression, staleness, frustration, and other problems
- get to understand and love each other
- become responsive to the Holy Spirit's dealing and obedient to God's Word
  and that's GROWTH.

How do you GROW a study group?

- Just start by asking a friend to join you and then aim at expanding your group.
- Study the set portions daily (they are brief and easy: no catches).
- Meet once a week to discuss what you find.
- Befriend others, both Christians and non Christians, and work away together
  see how it GROWS!

WHEN you GROW ...

This will happen at school, at home, at work, at play, in your youth group, your student fellowship, women's meetings, mid-week meetings, churches and communities,

you'll be REACHING THROUGH TEACHING

INTRODUCTORY STUDY

Joshua was a real person. He had to face problems, fears and difficulties just as you and I do.

• Do you find that, when you try to stick up for what is right, the opposition (either from family, friends or workmates) is hard to take?

Joshua found this too. Read about it in Numbers 14:1-7.
What did Joshua do? (Num. 14:7-9).

• Do you feel that your responsibilities just now are more than you can cope with?

So did Joshua. Read what he was asked to do, in Numbers 27:18-23.
How did God reassure him? (Josh. 1:9).

• Do you ever wonder if the promises in the Bible can really relate to you in your situation?

Joshua must have wondered too (Josh. 6:1, 2).
How did he find out if God's promise was true? (Josh. 6:3-7, 20).
Are you willing to prove God in this way?

• Are you prone to depression? And do you ever question whether God knows what He's doing?

Joshua went through this too (Josh. 7:6, 7).
What was God's remedy? (Josh. 7:10-12).
Read what Paul discovered (Rom. 7:18, 19, 24, 25).

The happenings of the Old Testament were real happenings.

Yet God has caused this book to be written, not merely to give us the history of a nation, but to teach us truths that are vital for us today.

Read together the story of God's dealings with His people, presented in a nutshell in Joshua 24:5-13.

Notice that God always takes the initiative.

This story is an analogy of the way God deals with an individual believer today.

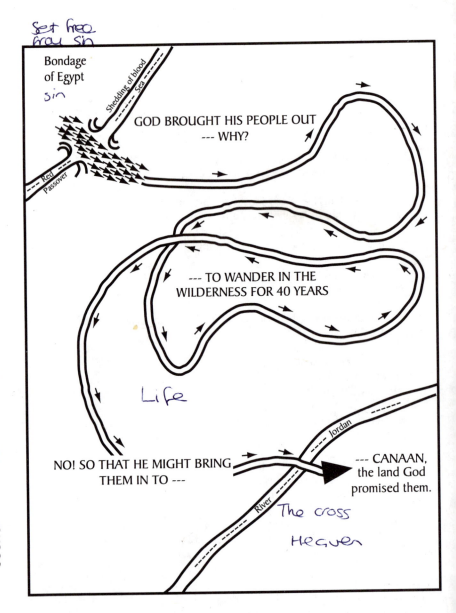

Set free from sin

Bondage of Egypt

sin

Shedding of blood

Sea

Red

Passover

GOD BROUGHT HIS PEOPLE OUT
--- WHY?

--- TO WANDER IN THE
WILDERNESS FOR 40 YEARS

Life

Jordan

NO! SO THAT HE MIGHT BRING
THEM IN TO ---

--- CANAAN,
the land God
promised them.

River

The cross

Heaven

Look at the diagram opposite:

For 'Egypt' write 'sin', and read Romans 8:2.
For 'Passover' write 'The Cross' and read I Peter 1:8-19.

DISCUSS:

When a person accepts that Christ died for him to free him from the bondage of sin and receives Christ into his life – what difference will it make to him?

What do you think 'the wilderness' represents in a Christian's life?

Now read Ephesians 1:18-20 and Hebrews 4:9-11 and discuss what Canaan represents in the analogy.

Write your answers on the diagram.

STUDY 1

THE MAN GOD CAN USE

DAY 1 a) We first read of Joshua as Moses' servant. What was Joshua doing in the following passages – Exodus 17:9-13; 24:12-14; 33:7-11; Numbers 13:16-20?
b) How did Joshua show his faith in God in the story told in Numbers 14:6-9?

DAY 2 *Numbers 27:15-23; Deuteronomy 31:1-8.*
a) Who did Moses tell the people would go with them into the promised land?
b) Deuteronomy 31:22-27. Who spoke to Joshua in Numbers 27:23? (LB inaccurate here)
c) What did Joshua see Moses doing?

DAY 3 *Exodus 3:16-17; Joshua 1:1-4.*
a) What had God promised Moses?
b) How did Joshua know it was time for him to take command?

DAY 4 *Joshua 1:5-7; Numbers 23:19.*
a) What promises did God give Joshua? How do you think Joshua felt?
b) How do we know that God still keeps His promises today? (e.g. Matt. 28:20).

DAY 5 *Joshua 1:8, 9; Psalm 1:1-3; Acts 17:11.*
a) What did God tell Joshua to do, that He always wants us to do?
b) Share with your group how the study of God's word is or has been a blessing to you.

DAY 6 *Joshua 1:5-9; John 8:29.*
a) How was it that both Jesus and Joshua were able to fulfil the tasks God gave them?
b) What did Jesus say He always did?
c) Which verse in Joshua chapter 1 shows that God told Joshua to do this too?

DAY 7 *Joshua 1:10-18.*
a) What were Joshua's instructions to the men of Reuben and Gad?
b) How did these men encourage their leader?

NOTES

Names were important in Old Testament days, and Joshua's parents had given him the name 'HOSHEA' which means 'SALVATION'. With God-given discernment, Moses changed his name to 'JE-HOSHEA' meaning 'God is salvation.'

WHAT DID GOD ASK JOSHUA TO DO?

After many years of happily being the servant of a great man, Joshua found himself moved into No. 1 position, commissioned to lead the people into the promised land.

How overwhelming! How nerve-wracking! 'How can I do it?' he must have thought. 'I can't even go to dear old Moses for advice! I feel inadequate.'

Have you ever felt like that? Perhaps someone is asking you right now to take a position of leadership or teaching in your church, or in Christian work. 'I couldn't possibly'– you say. 'I'll help someone else, but I couldn't take the lead.' You feel inadequate.

Well, you're just the kind of person the Lord is looking for! It's the right way to feel. Because when a person feels self-confident, he makes it difficult for the Lord to use him.

SO HOW DID JOSHUA GET ON?

The Lord spoke to him and said, 'Be strong! Be courageous!' Now He wasn't just saying, 'Pull your socks up, old chap. You can do it if you try.'

No, the Lord showed Joshua what he later taught Paul:

'I am with you; that is all you need. My power shows up best in weak people' (2 Cor. 12:9, LB).

'Great!' Joshua might have thought. 'I can go ahead and make my plans, and God has promised that He'll be with me, He'll never leave me, and I'll never be defeated.'

But, wait a minute, Joshua – that's not what God means.

God is the one who makes the plans,
God is the one who gives the commands, and
God is the one who will win the victories.

How significant was the change in Joshua's name from 'salvation' to 'God is Salvation'?

Have you realized this in your situation? God has a perfect plan for your life from this moment on. He knows exactly what He wants you to do day by day, and He will tell you. Also, it is God who will win the victories in your life, over sin and temptation. All He asks is that you are willing to let Him take control and that you rest in Him.

Doesn't it bring a tremendous sense of release when we grasp this truth? Ask God to teach you more about this principle of 'rest' as we continue these studies.

BUT HOW COULD JOSHUA DISCOVER GOD'S WILL?

It is interesting to note that up to this point of time in history God has spoken to His people in dreams and visions, or by angelic ministry. Before Moses died, however, he wrote down the Law of God and Joshua is instructed to become really familiar with it and obey it. God would be using a new method of teaching His people from now on – teaching them through the written Word.

Joshua's 'Bible' would have included only the first five books of Moses. How fortunate we are in having all the rest, especially the accounts of God's Son coming to earth to die for us and rise from the dead.

Hebrews 1:1 says:

'Long ago God spoke in many different ways to our fathers through the prophets ... but now in these days He has spoken to us through His Son.'

We, even more than Joshua, should do what God tells us when He says:

'This book of the law shall not depart out of your mouth, but you shall meditate on it day and night, that you may be careful to do according to all that is written in it' (Josh. 1:8, RSV).

STUDY 2
THE GRAIN OF MUSTARD SEED

QUESTIONS

When you get together as a group, first read the whole of chapter 2 as a play (you might even like to act it!). You will need a narrator, a King's messenger, Rahab, and 2 spies. Make sure your readers all have the same version. (Some versions have Joshua speaking in v. 1).

DAY 1 *Joshua 2:1-7.*
a) What was the first preparation Joshua made for the attack on Canaan?
b) What can you discover about Rahab from these verses?

DAY 2 *Joshua 2:8-14. (Read in Living Bible.)*
a) What startling discovery did the spies make?
b) How did Rahab show that she was different from the other people in Jericho? (see Luke 17:5, 6).

DAY 3 *Joshua 2:15-21.*
a) What made it easy for the spies to escape from the city?
b) What did Rahab do after the spies had gone?

DAY 4 *Joshua 2:9, 22-24; 6:16.*
a) What message did Rahab, then the spies, then Joshua pass on?
b) Since this was before the fall of Jericho, what did it show?

DAY 5 *Hebrews 11:31; James 2:21-25.*
a) For what is Rahab commended in Hebrews 11:31?
b) For what is she commended in James 2:25?
c) How would you explain the apparent contradiction?

DAY 6 *Joshua 6:20-25.*
a) When the two spies saw the walls collapsing, what might they have wondered (see 2:15)?
b) Where did they take Rahab and her family?

DAY 7 *Matthew 1:1, 5, 6.*
a) What can you find out about Rahab from these verses?
b) Luke 15:7. How does this link up with the story of Rahab?

NOTES

'It only takes a spark to get a fire going,
and soon all those around can warm up in its glowing.
That's how it is with God's love, once you've
experienced it, you spread His love to everyone,
you want to pass it on ... pass it on ....'

FAITH SO SMALL

Rahab's faith was no more that a mere spark, a tiny mustard seed. Imagine what this woman's life must have been like before this time – sordid, immoral and tragic; full of sensuality, fear and darkness. Then she heard about a God who was all-powerful, who rescued His people from bondage, protected them in their journeys, and defeated their enemies – and a glimmer of hope came into her sin-stained life.

When the army of this awe-inspiring God drew near her city she knew that only He could save her and her family from death and destruction, and she had faith enough to believe that He would.

FAITH BEING PASSED ON

That was all the faith she had, but look what she did with it. She passed it on. She said to the spies, 'I know that the Lord *has given* you this land.' The spies returned and told Joshua, 'We are sure that the Lord *has given* us the whole country.' Later Joshua said to the people of Israel, 'The Lord *has given* you the city!' Rahab's faith was being passed on.

FAITH IN ACTION

Rahab might have used the same words as the jailer at Philippi did when Paul was in prison there: 'What must I do to be saved?'

The answer for Rahab was that she was to put her faith completely in a piece of scarlet cord, trust her very life and the lives of her family to it. She could have said, 'What use is this scarlet cord? Can it really save me? I don't think I'll leave it hanging there any longer. Why, someone might climb up it!'

In the same way, the Israelites in Egypt might have said at Passover time, 'How can blood on our doorsteps possibly save us from death?'

Today, when some people consider the death of Jesus on the cross, the shedding of His blood for our redemption, they ask, 'How can something that happened 2,000 years ago have any relevance for me today?'

The reply to all these questions is that God has provided only ONE WAY to be saved
- The scarlet cord for Rahab.
- Blood on the doorposts for the Israelites.
  Both looking ahead to:

- The atoning death of Christ for you and me.

And if we refuse to put our faith in this, there is no other way.

FAITH TESTED
Can you imagine how Rahab must have felt when the city walls began to crumble? Remember her house was built into the wall! Did her friends and neighbours scream at her to come out? But she had to stay in the house – the house divinely protected by the scarlet cord. God was putting her faith to the test in a very exacting way, but she came through the test with flying colours. Her faith was also strong enough to convince her relations, so she must have been 'Passing it on'.

FAITH GROWING
Can't you imagine that it was a new and different Rahab who was taken away from her old life of sin to safety beside the camp of God's people? What a testimony she would have! I'm sure she was eager to find out all she could about the wonderful God who had saved her because she trusted Him. And her faith would grow and grow as she witnessed what God continued to do – those events which we shall be studying in the book of Joshua.

FAITH FITTING IN TO GOD'S PLAN
Our last glimpse of Rahab shows her as a happy naturalized Israelite wife and mother. She married a man called Salmon, of the tribe of Judah, whose father had been a wealthy leader of this respected tribe. Rahab bore a son whom they called Boaz, and as a boy he must have heard many times the exciting story of how his mother had been rescued from Jericho.

Once again she had opportunity to pass on her faith.

Boaz grew up to be a fine, godly man (as we can read in the book of Ruth) and Rahab, had she known it, was destined to be the great-great-grandmother of King David, from whose line was born the Son of God.

What is God saying to you through the life of Rahab?

'Pass it on....'

STUDY 3
IS YOUR FAITH GOING FORWARD?

QUESTIONS

DAY 1 *Joshua 3:1-4.*
a) What did the leaders tell the people to do? Why?
b) How is it that Jesus can show us the way through our problems and temptations (Heb. 2:18; 4:15, 16)?

DAY 2 *Joshua 3:5, 6; 2 Corinthians 7:1.*
a) What did Joshua tell the people to do? Why?
b) What are we told to do, as people of God?

DAY 3 *Joshua 3:7, 8; Hebrews 12:2.*
a) What would the people be looking at as the priests led the way forward?
b) What are we advised to do in our daily life? How will this help us?

DAY 4 *2 Corinthians 5:7; Galatians 2:20 (read in several versions.)*
a) Explain the Corinthians verse.
b) How does Paul say he lives his life?

DAY 5 *Joshua 3:9-13.*
a) What were the people to learn that day, that is also found in Isaiah 43:2?
b) How was the faith of the priests going to be tested?

DAY 6 *Joshua 3:14-17.*
a) Why was this not the best time to attempt the crossing of the Jordan?
b) Hebrews 11:29 tells of the crossing of the Red Sea. How did the Israelites get through, and why did the Egyptians not?

DAY 7 *Joshua 3:1-17.*
a) How many times is the Ark of the Covenant (or Covenant box) mentioned in this chapter? What do you think this shows us?
b) What has impressed you most in this study?

NOTES

How does faith 'Go Forward'? God tells us to walk by faith and to live by faith, and these are pictures of forward movement and growth. When we find ourselves with a problem, we have an opportunity to exercise our faith and to prove the Lord and consequently our faith will go forward. Also, we will have something to share with others about how God has dealt with our problem.

The people of Israel were faced with an impossible situation. Really impossible. How could some 2.5 million people (including children and babies), with all their belongings and livestock, possibly get across a deep, flooded, fast-flowing river? Humanly speaking, they couldn't. It was quite impossible.

Are you facing an impossible situation in your life?

A problem that seems to have no way through?

Let's interview some of the Israelites standing there on the east bank of the Jordan, and see how they are feeling.

Perhaps we can discover from them something that would help us today.

INTERVIEWER:	Excuse me, sir, would you mind answering some questions?
SHAPAT:	Not at all. What do you want to know?.
INTERVIEWER:	Well, how long has this huge crowd of people been here on the banks of the river?
SHAPAT:	We have been camping here for 3 days now.
INTERVIEWER:	How much longer do you expect to stay?
SHAPAT:	Only until tomorrow.
INTERVIEWER:	Oh. Where do you go then?
SHAPAT:	Tomorrow we shall cross the Jordan and enter the land that God has promised to His people. What an exciting day that will be!
INTERVIEWER:	Cross the Jordan? How? Have you boats to carry everyone?
SHAPAT:	Oh no!
INTERVIEWER:	Well, you would hardly get a bridge built in that time. Or can everyone swim? What about the children?
SHAPAT:	No no, it won't be like that at all.
INTERVIEWER:	Well, how ...?
SHAPAT:	We don't know exactly. But you see, God knows all about it. He has brought us this far and has promised us the land of Canaan, so He would hardly leave us to work this out on our own – now would He?
INTERVIEWER:	I – I suppose not.
HELEK:	Joshua told us that the Lord will perform a miracle for us tomorrow. So perhaps He will roll back the waters when Joshua holds out his stick, like Moses did with our fathers at the Red Sea.
SHAPAT:	It will be interesting to see how God will solve our problem, but it does not really matter how He does it. We know He will and we just have to

	be ready to do what He tells us.
INTERVIEWER:	You seem very confident about it.
HELEK:	We are. You see, when we were camping at Shittim some of us did have misgivings about crossing the river. Oh, we trusted God all right, but we talked about it among ourselves and kept going to look at the river and wondering what was the best way to tackle it.
SHAPAT:	I had even made some plans myself and I wondered if God would do it my way – but I see now it wouldn't have worked.
HELEK:	Then Joshua came along. He's a great leader and God is with him in just the same way as He was with Moses. He reminded us that God is with all of us all of the time, and he told us to stop looking at the river and worrying, and instead to keep our eyes on the Ark of the Covenant and trust ourselves completely to the Lord.
INTERVIEWER:	Now – How would looking at the Ark help you?
SHAPAT:	Well, for a start, none of us has been through anything like this before, so we had to have someone who would guide us. The more we look at the Ark, the more we remember how wonderful our God is. Just think of all the mighty acts He has done in the past! We have every reason to be confident that He can and will find a way across this river for us.
INTERVIEWER:	That's great. I do admire your complete trust in God. A faith like that will really go forward and I can certainly see that it is the only way to deal with problems. Thank you so much for this interview.
SHAPAT:	A pleasure. May I ask you one question? Is your faith going forward?

STUDY 4
REMEMBER ... IT'S SO EASY TO FORGET!

QUESTIONS

DAY 1 *Joshua 3:8; 4:1-3, 15, 16.*
During this memorable day, the Lord gave Joshua 3 commands. What were they?

DAY 2 *Joshua 3:9-13; 4:4-7, 15-17.*
To whom did Joshua pass on each of the commands that the Lord had given him?

DAY 3 *Joshua 3:15-17; 4:8-10, 18.*
a) Which of the 3 commands were carried out exactly as the Lord had said?
b) Where did Joshua set up a pile of stones?

DAY 4 *Joshua 3:7; 4:10-14; Matthew 23:11, 12.*
a) How did the people regard Joshua after this unforgettable day?
b) What was God's purpose in allowing this to happen?

DAY 5 *Joshua 4:6, 7, 19-24; 5:1.*
a) When future generations would ask what the pile of stones at Gilgal was for, what was to be the reply?
b) What would result from this?
c) What was the immediate reaction of the Amorite and Canaanite kings?

DAY 6 *Psalm 114:1-7; Ephesians 1:19, 20.*
a) If you could again interview Shapat and Helek (see last week's notes) at the end of this great day, what might they say to you?
b) What was the greatest ever demonstration of God's power?

DAY 7 *Joshua 5:2-12; Genesis 17:10-14; Exodus 13:5.*
a) Of what was circumcision a sign?
b) What else did the people do at Gilgal?
c) What is there in Exodus 12:21-27 that reminds you of Day 5 readings?

NOTES

'Is this Gilgal now, Dad?'

'Yes, my son, this is Gilgal.'

'The very special place you said we'd visit?'

'That's right.'

'What's that over there, Dad?'

'It's a pile of 12 stones.'

'A pile of stones? I thought it might be something special.'

'It is special, lad. This is what we came to see.'

'Oh! Then what do these stones mean? Where did they come from?'

'Well, son, when I was a lad about your age, the people of Israel did not live here in Canaan, as we do now. We lived in tents, on the other side of the Jordan. Then one day God told Joshua that we were going to cross the river and enter this land, which He had promised to His people years back.'

'What a day that was! I'll never forget the excitement. The priests carrying the Ark of the Covenant went first, and as soon as they stepped into the river the Lord God dried up the water, and kept the riverbed dry until all of us had crossed over.'

'Wow! I always knew God was great and powerful, but I didn't know He could do that! But what about these stones? Where did they come in?'

'They didn't come in, son, they came out! Out of the middle of the River Jordan. Joshua chose 12 men to carry one stone each from the place where the priests were standing.'

'It's a wide river, isn't it and it's very deep. So they could never have taken these stones out unless the water had stopped flowing. Isn't that something? These very stones here lay for centuries at the bottom of the river and now they are on dry land!'

'Yes and they are here for a purpose. When we look at these stones, we remember God's great power and His faithfulness to His people. Don't forget what I've told you, son, and when you grow up and become a father, you tell your children about this too.'

'I will, Dad. I'll tell the boys when I get back home that I've seen and even touched the Gilgal stones!'

THE STONES were a reminder of God's great power and the people's complete dependence on Him.

THE PASSOVER was also a reminder of God's great power and the people's complete dependence on Him. God said, 'Celebrate this day to remind you of what I, the Lord, have done' (Exod. 12:14).

But the greatest demonstration of God's power was the death and resurrection of our Lord Jesus Christ. He commanded us to keep the reality of these events fresh in our minds by remembering.

JOSHUA • STUDY 4 • REMEMBER ... IT'S SO EASY TO FORGET!

THE LORD'S SUPPER when He said, 'Do this in remembrance of Me.'

We are reminded of our complete dependence on Him for salvation and we are told to teach our children about this memorial 'until He comes'.

How would you answer if someone asked you, 'What does the Lord's Supper mean to you?'

> Thy body broken for my sake,
> my bread from heaven shall be,
> thy testamental cup I take
> and thus remember Thee.
>
> When to the Cross I turn my eyes
> and rest on Calvary,
> O Lamb of God, my sacrifice,
> I must remember Thee.
>
> Remember Thee, and all Thy pains
> and all Thy love to me,
> Yes, while a breath, a pulse remains,
> I will remember Thee.'

STUDY 5
ALLOW GOD COMPLETE CONTROL

QUESTIONS

DAY 1 *Joshua 5:13-15; 6:2.*
a) Gilgal was 5 kilometres from Jericho. Why do you think Joshua had gone over to the city?
b) Whom did he meet?

DAY 2 *Joshua 5:14, 15; 2 Kings 6:11-17; Matthew 26:53.*
a) What did the man mean by 'The Lord's army'?
b) Exodus 3:4-6; Psalm 95:6. How did Joshua respond when the man told him who He was?

DAY 3 *Joshua 6:1-5; 2 Chronicles 20:15, 17.*
a) What were the orders the Lord gave Joshua?
b) How did these orders show that the battle was to be the Lord's?

DAY 4 *Joshua 6:6-11; I Corinthians 1:27-29.*
a) Imagine you are one of the people in Jericho. How would you feel as you watched the Israelites?
b) Think of other examples of how God used what the world would consider foolish, to accomplish His purposes.

DAY 5 *Joshua 6:12-21; I Samuel 17:47; Zechariah 4:6.*
a) Draw a diagram of the Israelites surrounding the city, as if seen from the air. What does the end of verse 20 describe?
b) How does the Lord win His victories?

DAY 6 *2 Corinthians 10:4; Ephesians 6:10-12, 17, 18; Hebrews 11:30.*
a) Against whom are we, as Christians, fighting?
b) What weapons can we use?

DAY 7 *Joshua 6:22-27; Genesis 15:16; I Kings 16:34.*
a) Why did the Lord order Jericho to be destroyed?
b) What people were saved?
c) What things were salvaged?

NOTES

THE PROBLEM

Joshua had a problem, an impossible situation, as he approached the fortified city of Jericho on the hill and considered it. Was he trying to decide how to overcome the problem? What tactics to use? Did he have to admit there seemed to be no solution?

When you have read this far, stop for 2 or 3 minutes. Close your eyes and each of you think to yourself of one problem confronting you at present.

THE MAN

Suddenly, Joshua saw a man standing in front of him. We can understand how Joshua's mind was ticking over. There would be two sides in the forthcoming battle – the enemy and the Israelites so he asked, 'Whose side are you on?'

The man replied in effect, 'I have not come to take sides, I have come to take over. I want to have complete control.'

Recognizing the Lord, Joshua immediately gave the whole situation over to Him, saying, 'What do you want me to do?'

As you pause here, ask yourself if you are willing to allow the Lord to have complete control of your problem. That means 'hands off' no matter what happens. It's His problem now, so don't worry any more, or plan or work out solutions any more or even to pray and plead with Him about it any more. This is what 'resting in Jesus' means.
It is standing aside from the problem, waiting for God to act. All you need to do now is to ask, 'What do you want me to do?' Are you willing?

THE STRATEGY

Joshua got his orders. Oh dear, isn't this going to make him look rather foolish? This wasn't the sort of thing he would have planned. All this walking, then waiting, day after day, with nothing happening. Does God really know what He's doing?

It would have been much easier to get out those weapons of war and attack the city, asking God for help. But that is never God's way and Joshua was willing to trust Him completely.

Isn't that often where we miss out? We forget that we are fighting against the spiritual forces behind our problems, so we try to puzzle out solutions on the human level. We even tell God what we want Him to do! But we can only conquer with spiritual weapons such as faith, righteousness and prayer.

Are you willing to trust God even when nothing seems to be happening and others think you're crazy?

THE VICTORY

One of the most important lessons God teaches us right through the Bible is this:

Victory for the Christian comes only from total dependence on God.

God's way of victory for Joshua was marching round Jericho.

– for David,	It was a sling and a stone.
– for Gideon,	A handful of men against a vast army.
– for Elijah,	One man versus the rest.
– for Daniel,	The lions' den.
– for Paul,	Physical weakness.
– for Jesus,	The Cross.

God's ways are not our ways (and this is one of the most difficult lessons to learn) but God's ways are always best.

Do you really believe this?

Look expectantly to Him and see what His way of victory is for you in your particular problem.

Can you honestly pray this prayer?

Lord God, Almighty and All-powerful, I hand over my problem completely to You. Lord, You already know how You will solve this problem, and I trust You absolutely for the outcome. Your ways are always best, and I am content to do whatever You want me to do.

STUDY 6
DOING THINGS OUR OWN WAY

QUESTIONS

DAY 1 *Joshua 6:17,18; 7:1-5.*
a) What was the people's suggestion about how to attack Ai?
b) What happened?
c) What was the Israelites' reaction?

DAY 2 *Joshua 7:6-9; Proverbs 3:5, 6.*
a) What did Joshua and the leaders do now, that they had forgotten to do before attacking Ai?
b) What were they afraid would happen? (Read Deut. 11:22, 23).

DAY 3 *Joshua 7:10-15; Luke 12:15; Romans 1:18; Hebrews 13:5; 1 Timothy 6:9, 10.*
a) What did God show them was the reason for their defeat?
b) What does the Bible tell us is the source (or root) of all kinds of evil?

DAY 4 *Joshua 7:16-26; Genesis 3:6; 1 John 2:16.*
a) What had Achan taken for himself?
b) What were the 4 steps by which Achan described his disobedience?
c) What can we learn about the character of Jesus from Mark 9:42-50?

DAY 5 *Joshua 8:1-9.*
a) What was the Lord's plan for the attack on Ai?
b) How were His instructions about the contents of the city different from those concerning Jericho?

DAY 6 *Joshua 8:10-17.*
a) Draw a diagram showing the position of: the city, the men in ambush, the main part of Joshua's army, the King of Ai and his men.
b) Why did the men of Ai leave the city unprotected?

DAY 7 *Joshua 8:18-29; Exodus 14:16.*
a) What signal did Joshua make to show God was giving him the city?
b) How did the men of Ai find themselves cornered?

NOTES

ACHAN did things his own way and brought down the terrible wrath of God upon himself.

THE ISRAELITES did things their own way, and only by immediately searching themselves to find out the sin in their nation did they escape the judgement of God.

'Sin' just means 'doing things our own way' not God's way and sin brings its dreadful consequences, if not in this life then in the life after death. All sin is against God and He cannot be indifferent to it. His judgment must fall on those who sin against Him.

- Remember the people in Noah's day?

'When the Lord saw how wicked everyone on earth was and how evil their thoughts were all the time... He said, "I will wipe out these people I have created"' (Gen. 6:5-7).

- And Lot's heavenly visitors?

'We are going to destroy this place. The Lord has heard the terrible accusations against these people and has sent us to destroy Sodom.... Suddenly the Lord rained burning sulphur on the cities of Sodom and Gomorrah and destroyed them, and the whole valley, along with all the people there' (Gen. 19:13, 24, 25).

As regards the people living in the land of Canaan in Joshua's day, they were so sunken in sin and so given up to vices of a most degrading nature that God's flaming sword of justice had to be unsheathed. Spiritual evil had taken complete control of them and their time for punishment had now come.

So the Israelites were the instrument by which God inflicted judgement, because of the depravity of these people. In those times the motives for destruction and slaughter were looting or revenge but God imposed a moral restraint on His people to show them that these were not to be their motives, but rather that they were the instrument of punishment in His hand.

Also, the Israelites had been chosen by God as the nation that was to bring God's message of salvation to the world. He had promised them a land of their own but they must remove all possibility of infection by heathen religions if they were to be kept pure and true to Him.

Certainly, the means of removing the dreaded infection was a drastic one but like a cancerous growth it had to be completely cut out. Nothing less would do. Sadly we find that where this command of the Lord was not fully obeyed, the Canaanites who were left (even though they became slaves) were the cause of Israel falling into sin again and again.

* * *

When we read such accounts of wholesale slaughter in the Old Testament, we naturally ask: 'Is such a revelation of God's character consistent with the revelation of the Father that Jesus has given us ?'

Consider these words of the Lord:

'If anyone will not receive you or listen to what you say, then as you leave that house or that town, shake the dust of it off your feet. I tell you this: on the day of judgment it will be more bearable for the land of Sodom and Gomorrah than for that town' (Matt. 10 :14, 15).

'The Kingdom of heaven is like a king who prepared a banquet ...then the king told his attendants, 'Tie him hand and foot and throw him outside into the darkness, where there will be weeping and grinding of teeth" (Matt. 22:2, 13).

'How terrible for you teachers of the Law and Pharisees! Hypocrites! You sail the seas and cross whole countries to win one convert, and when you succeed, you make him twice as deserving of going to hell as you yourselves are' (Matt. 23:15).

'Then I will turn to those on my left hand and say: "Away with you, you cursed ones, into the eternal fire prepared for the devil and his demons"' (Matt. 25:41).

Jesus showed very clearly God the Father's horror and hatred of sin and also that a just God must punish those who break His laws. He would not be a God of justice if He did not react in this way.

So the lesson which God teaches us so dramatically in the Old Testament, He continues to teach us in the New Testament, and we must realize that in our own lives 'doing things our own way' calls down God's wrath. It is as serious as that.

STUDY 7

RIGHT? – OR WRONG?

QUESTIONS

DAY 1 *Deuteronomy 27:1-8; Joshua 8:30-32.*
a) Where did Joshua build the altar?
b) Where had he been instructed to write out the Law of Moses?
c) How was he to write them?

DAY 2 *Deuteronomy 11:29-32; 27:11-14; Joshua 8:33.*
a) From which mountain were the curses to be read? And which the blessings?
b) How many tribes were to stand on each mountain?
c) What was to be in between?
Try to picture the scene.

DAY 3 *Joshua 8:34, 35; Deuteronomy 27:15-26; 28:1-9.*
a) From the list of curses, which ones are particularly relevant in our society today?
b) Why do you think the people were to answer 'Amen'?

DAY 4 *Joshua 9:1-13; Exodus 23:31-33; Deuteronomy 7:2.*
a) What had God commanded that His people should not do?
b) What was the plan by which the Gibeonites hoped to deceive the Israelite leaders and cause them to disobey God?

DAY 5 *Joshua 9:14-21.*
a) How was it that the Israelites fell into the trap?
b) What do you think God's command in 2 Corinthians 6:14, 15 means for us today?

DAY 6 *Joshua 9:22-27.*
a) What was the curse pronounced on the Gibeonites?
b) Why did the Israelites not kill them (see vv. 15, 18-20)?

DAY 7 *Deuteronomy 30:15-19; Amos 5:14, 15; John 10:10.*
a) What was the choice offered to the people?
b) Romans 12:9; 1 Thessalonians 5:21-24. Some people today say there is no such a thing as 'right' or 'wrong' – it depends on your situation. How would you answer them?

NOTES

Do you know what a 'mugwump' is? Originally an Indian Chief of great importance, too grand to take sides, it has come to mean 'one who sits on the fence'.

Now the Lord made sure there was no fence to sit on between Mt. Ebal and Mt. Gerizim! No mugwumps were catered for. Because the way God has planned things, there are only two categories of people in His sight:

Those who have chosen life and those who have chosen death.
Those who are right with God and those who are not right with God.
Those enjoying God's blessing and those under God's curse.
Those who obey God and those who disobey God.

Similarly, in daily life, God shows us that certain things are right, while other things are wrong.

This was what He wanted to impress upon His people soon after they came into the promised land and what a dramatic way He chose to do it.

With the sound of the blessings and cursings in their ears, the people came down from the mountains and proceeded to get on with everyday living.

RIGHT   Of course they would obey all of God's laws!
Of course they were eager to put them into practice!
'All that the Lord has spoken we will do.'

And what is the next episode in the story?

WRONG   They allied themselves with the people of the land.
They did exactly what God had forbidden.
'But they were deceived,' you say, 'They wouldn't have signed the treaty if they had known.'

Oh yes, but Satan the deceiver is very cunning! He breaks through the believer's armour whenever he sees the smallest chink. And in this case, the chink was prayerlessness – not keeping in touch with God.

Does Satan ever pierce your armour at this point?

If we are to know what is right and what is wrong in every situation, we must keep in touch constantly with our God.

Once we neglect this, Satan will be in with his tricks.

How can we know the will of God?

What is right and what is wrong?

The Bible says: 'Offer yourselves as a living sacrifice to God, dedicated to his service and pleasing to him ... let God transform you inwardly.... Then you will be able to know the will of God –' (Rom. 12:1, 2, GNB)

STUDY 8
WHO WINS THE VICTORIES?

QUESTIONS

DAY 1 *Joshua 1:3-6.*
a) What 3 promises did God give to Joshua when he first became the leader of the people?
b) Read Hebrews 4:9-11 carefully in several translations including the Good News Bible. What is the 'rest' which God promises here (see also notes on Study 5)?

DAY 2 *Joshua 10:1-8; I Corinthians 15:57.*
a) What did we read last week about the people of Gibeon?
b) What was their problem now?
c) What promise did God give Joshua about this?

DAY 3 *Joshua 10:9-15; Nehemiah 4:20.*
What 5 things are we told about the Lord in these passages?

DAY 4 *Joshua 10:16-27; Ephesians 6:12; Colossians 3:5, 8.*
a) In what way is this section a picture of the Christian life?
b) How did Joshua encourage his officers?

DAY 5 *Joshua 10:28-43.*
a) What is made very clear in verses 30, 32 and 42?
b) Look at the map, if possible, to locate the area of these conquests. What would the Israelites be reminded of every time they returned to Gilgal (v. 43. See also v. 15, and 4:19, 20)?

DAY 6 *Joshua 11:1-11.*
a) How is the army from the north described here? (Hazor is north of the sea of Galilee).
b) Why would the Israelites be particularly afraid of this army?
c) What gave them confidence?

DAY 7 *Joshua 11:12-23; John 17:4; I Corinthians 15:25.*
a) What lessons can you learn from verse 15?
b) This chapter marks the end of the united attacks of the Israelites against the people of Canaan. What has helped you most in this week's study?

NOTES

The book of Joshua is a history book, recording the takeover of the land of Canaan by the Israelites. Yet it is different from other histories of battles and conquests because it shows very clearly that the Lord God was doing the fighting, and His people simply obeyed.

This is the principle referred to in the New Testament as: 'Entering into His Rest' (Heb. 4:10).

If you count the number of times the Lord's Name is mentioned in this week's study, you will find that it appears 20 times. If you look closely to find out what is said about the Lord in these 20 references, you will see that He is active and busy on behalf of His people.

Jesus said later, 'My Father works, and I work.'

It is a fallacy of today – even among Christians – to imagine that God is a kind of passive Being who sits benignly in Heaven watching His people! We are so busy fighting our own battles, that we don't stop to consider how active God is all the time, in and around us.

So let's learn something positive from Joshua this week, and be alert to see how our God, who is the same yesterday, today and for ever, fights for His people.

I. THE LORD SAID, 'DON'T BE AFRAID OF THEM ... FOR I ...' (10:8; 11:6)
This is how God begins His work – through His Word.

Try to realize the importance of getting to know God's Word thoroughly, of reading as much of it as you can as often as you can; thinking about it, and praying that God will help you to apply it to yourself. Then you will find encouragement, as Joshua did, and hope and strength for the tasks ahead.

God is not just saying 'Don't worry', but He gives the reason why ...'for I have given you the victory.'

This is what it means to trust God completely, to take Him at His word, believing He has the problem under control.

2. THE LORD WAS FIGHTING FOR ISRAEL (10:14, 25, 42; 11:20)
Are there times when you feel you are fighting a losing battle? Perhaps it is a battle of relationships or a battle of depression or even despair; or fear or insecurity; or a battle against impatience, bad temper, impure thoughts.

Remember the soldier doesn't go to his commanding officer and say, 'Please help me to fight this battle' – no, he waits for his orders and then concentrates on obeying, knowing that the officer plans the strategy which will conquer the enemy.

So it is with us. The Lord does not expect us to be able to cope with the enemies of depression, selfishness, bitterness and all the rest by ourselves, but He promises to fight for us.

3. THE LORD PERFORMED MIRACLES (10:10, 11, 12-14)

The Israelites couldn't miss seeing the miracles of the hailstorm and the sun standing still, but do you notice when the Lord works miracles in your life? Has He changed you from a quick-tempered, sharp-tongued person into one who has a real love for others? Has He transformed you from someone who was critical and bitter into someone who delights in fellowship around the Word of God?

This kind of miracle is much greater and more dramatic in God's sight than altering the course of nature, for by it He has gained the victory He most desires – a soul won over to Himself.

4. THE LORD GAVE THE ISRAELITES VICTORY (10:12, 19, 30, 32; 11:8)

These two chapters sparkle with this gem of truth. It shines through again and again and we are left in no doubt as to WHO was responsible for defeating the enemy.

Will you grasp this jewel and carry it with you?

Appropriate it, so that you never forget that when a victory is won in your life, 'It is the Lord's doing; and it is marvellous in our eyes' (Ps. 118:23).

Strive for victory over sin, fight the good fight of faith, resist the devil ... but remember to give God the glory.

5. THIS IS WHAT THE LORD COMMANDED (10:40; 11:9, 15, 23)

The Lord commanded that the idolatrous people of the land were to be destroyed, as their time of judgement had come.

He commanded that the evil should be driven out of the land which He had promised to His people.

The Lord has also commanded that we should drive out of our lives those things that are not pleasing to Him, so that we might be the kind of people He wants us to be.

In your heart enthrone Him,	Crown Him as your Captain
There let Him subdue	In temptation's hour,
All that is not holy,	Let His will enfold you
All that is not true.	In its light and power.

STUDY 9
LOOKING BACK ... LOOKING FORWARD

QUESTIONS

DAY 1 *Joshua 12:1-6; Numbers 21:21-24, 33-35.*
a) LOOKING BACK. What happened when the people of Israel wanted to pass through the land of King Sihon? and of King Og? – A giant where they brothers?
b) Who was the leader of the people at this time?

DAY 2 *Joshua 12:7-24; 9:1-2; 10:1-5; 11:1-5.*
a) Were the Israelites on the attack or on the defence in the battles referred to in these readings?
b) How many 'Kings' (cities) had the Israelites conquered at this stage?

DAY 3 *Joshua 13:1-7.*
a) LOOKING FORWARD. What did the Lord tell Joshua?
b) What was he to do next?
c) Share with your group some way in which the Lord has clearly led you to do something.

DAY 4 *Joshua 13:8-14, 33; 14:4.*
a) What did the Levites not receive?
b) What did they receive?

DAY 5 *Numbers 18:8-20 (read v. 20 in Good News Bible); Deuteronomy 18:1-8.*
a) What promises did God give to Aaron and his descendants (the Levites) in the days of Moses? (note: Num. 18:20)
b) What are some of the promises God has given you today, if you are His child? e.g., Matthew 6:30-33; 2 Corinthians 12:9; 1 Peter 2:9. Can you think of others?

DAY 6 *Joshua 13:15-32.*
Make a rough sketch of the land of Israel with the river Jordan linking the Sea of Galilee and the Dead Sea. Divide the land east of the river into 3 sections; south (v. 16), middle (v. 27), and north (v. 30), and write the names of the tribes who settled there.

DAY 7 *Joshua 14:1-5.*
a) Who divided up the land west of the Jordan and how was it done?
b) How does God want us to live so that we, too, can receive what He has promised (Heb. 6:11-12)?

NOTES

This part of our study is rather like 'Ringing out the Old Year' and 'Ringing in the New'.

Joshua is looking back, recording what has already been achieved: great things, victories over formidable enemies, territory gained. Surely it would have been understandable if he had sat back and said, 'We're in the Promised Land ... We've arrived!'

It is good for us as Christians, to look back on what the Lord has done for us. He died for us, He redeemed us and He has brought us into a personal relationship with Himself. We love to sing,

> 'My sins are all forgiven,
> I'm on my way to Heaven,
> My heart is bubbling over
> With this joy, joy, joy.'

We've made it ... so we can relax!

But this isn't God's purpose for His people. He stands by us, as He stood by Joshua, and says, 'THERE IS STILL MUCH LAND TO BE TAKEN' or, in the words of the New Testament, 'LET US GO FORWARD TO MATURITY' (Heb. 6:1).

Bishop Alf Stanway, returning after a full and satisfying life of missionary service in Africa, could say at the age of 64:

'The Christian life is never a looking backward, but always a looking forward, and it is true for the Christian, if he wants to walk with God, that "The best is yet to be".'

'Life gets better, year by year. You are a little bit nearer home. You have more experience of God and Christ, more evidence of His mercy and His grace. You are more sure of His promises, more certain of the things that matter; less attached to things that pass and perish with the using.'

Paul gave us some graphic pictures of this when he wrote:

'One thing I do, forgetting what lies behind, and straining forward to what lies ahead, I press on toward the goal' (Phil. 3:13, 14, RSV).

'Though our outer nature is wasting away, our inner nature is being renewed every day' (2 Cor. 4:16, RSV).

'And as the Spirit of the Lord works within us, we become more and more like him' (2 Cor. 3:18, LB).

Can't you sense his excitement as he looks forward?

'I do not claim that I have already succeeded, or have already become perfect. I keep striving to win the prize...' (Phil. 3:12, GNB).

God told Joshua exactly what territories remained to be possessed. What areas of land need to be appropriated in your life?

Is your Quiet Time all you would like it to be?
Do you want to learn more about prayer?
Do you long for power over temptation?
Are you unsure about how to share your faith?
Do you want to be more effective in your service for the Lord?

Search His Word for the blessings He has promised you in Christ and ask HIM to reveal them to you, for there are many. Then, looking forward, claim those blessings and possess that land in His strength, so that you may be of service to Him to the very end.

'The Holy Spirit is the guarantee that we shall receive what God has promised his people...' (Eph. 1:14, Good News Bible)

STUDY 10
THE MAN WHO WAS DIFFERENT

QUESTIONS

DAY 1 *Numbers 13:1-3, 21-33; 14:1-10, 24.*
a) These readings tell what happened 45 years previously. What report did the majority of the spies bring back?
b) What was the attitude of Joshua and Caleb?
c) What promise did the Lord make to Caleb (14:24)?

DAY 2 *Joshua 14:6-15.*
a) What request did Caleb make to Joshua?
b) 1. How old was he when God promised him the land?
   2. How old was he now?

DAY 3 *Joshua 14:8,9,14; Numbers 14:24; 32:12.*
Read these verses over and over, and use several versions to enrich your study.
a) What can you find out about Caleb?
b) How was he different?
c) What is God saying to you as you ponder these verses?

DAY 4 *Joshua 14:12; 15:13-19.*
a) How did Caleb prove that God was true to His Word? (Compare Num. 13:33 and 14:9 with Josh. 15:14.)
b) What did Caleb's daughter ask for as a wedding present?

DAY 5 *Joshua 15:20, 63; 16:1, 10; 17:1, 12-13. (You can also read the verses in between if you like.)*
a) Which tribes are mentioned here?
b) How was Caleb (from the verses read yesterday) different from these people?

DAY 6 *Joshua 17:1-6; Numbers 27:1-7.*
a) Why did the 5 daughters of Zelophehad ask for a part of the land for themselves?
b) Who had originally commanded that they should be given the land?

DAY 7 *Joshua 17:14-18.*
a) Why did the descendants of Joseph ask for more land?
b) What were they told to do?

NOTES

Try to imagine the scene!

Twelve weary men are returning after 6 weeks of spying out the land of Canaan. Ten of them are discouraged and fearful. Humanly speaking, it would be impossible to capture the land. Two men, however, are different: enthusiastic and optimistic. Caleb is the spokesman.

10 spies:	'The people are powerful and their cities are very large and well fortified.'
Caleb:	'We should attack now. We are strong enough to conquer them.'
10 spies:	'The land doesn't even produce enough for the people who live there.'
Caleb:	'That's a lie! The land is rich and fertile.'
The people:	'The Lord hates us. He brought us out of Egypt just to hand us over to these Amorites, so that they could kill us. Wouldn't it be better to go back to Egypt?
Caleb:	'Do not rebel against the Lord. If the Lord is pleased with us, He will take us there.'
10 spies:	'Everyone we saw was very tall and we even saw giants there, the descendants of Anak.'
Caleb:	'The Lord is with us and has defeated the gods that protect them, so don't be afraid.'

Later .....

'Joshua blessed Caleb and gave him the city of Hebron as his possession. Caleb drove the descendants of Anak out of the city'

* * *

How was Caleb different?

1. *His faith was based on God's Word,* not on his own ability.
It was obvious that the people of Israel could not conquer the enemy in their own strength, but God had said, 'Go in and possess the land. Don't be afraid, I will fight for you.' Caleb refused to let go of God's promises, while the rest of the people were plunged into despair.

2. *He brought back an honest report.* No half-truths for Caleb, he was straight-forward in all he said. The other spies changed things to suit themselves and exaggerated the difficulties because they were scared and didn't want to enter the land. Caleb trusted the Lord so he had no reason to falsify the report.

3. *He 'wholly followed the Lord'.* What a statement!
Can you honestly say this about yourself? If you claim to be a Christian, you should be able to describe yourself in this way, for a Christian is one who is totally committed to Jesus Christ. If there is any part of your life not yielded to Him, this is sin and it is just as bad as the rebellion of the people of Israel. Search your heart today, confess your sin and hand over everything to Jesus and you too will be recorded in His Book as one who 'wholly follows the Lord'.

4. *He did not doubt God's promise.* It is one thing to claim the promises of God in a day of spiritual excitement and blessing, but when our feet are firmly on the ground again, how easily we can be made to doubt! If ever people poured cold water on a person's enthusiasm for God, it was when the 12 spies returned with their reports. Just think how the devil attacked Caleb through his well-meaning friends:

They said:	'Listen to reason, Caleb. God expects us to use the intelligence He has given us and not to fly in the face of danger.'
God said:	'Go in and possess the land.'
They said:	'Don't you care about the rest of us? We'll all be killed and our wives and children taken captive.'
God said:	'Go in and possess the land.'
They said:	'The fellow is crazy! How can he imagine he is a match for these giants?'
God said:	'Go in and possess the land.'
They said:	'We've got a better idea, Caleb. Let's go back to Egypt, at least we were safe there.'
God said:	'Go in and possess the land.'

Not only did Caleb stake everything on God's promise at that time, but he refused to let go of the promise for 45 years.

That's a long time and it reminds us of what was later written of Abraham:

'He did not doubt God's promise. He was absolutely sure that God would be able to do what He had promised' (Rom. 4:20, 21, GNB).

God is looking for people who are different, in the way that Caleb was. Will you be a volunteer? God says to every Christian:

'Don't let the world around you squeeze you into its own mould, but let God remould your minds from within' (Rom. 12:2, Phillips).

STUDY 11
DIVIDING THE LAND

QUESTIONS

DAY 1 *Joshua 18:1-10.*
a) What was the challenge that Joshua gave to the people of Israel at this stage?
b) What did he appoint men to do?

DAY 2 *Joshua 18:11; 19:1, 10, 17, 24, 32, 40; Deuteronomy 33:18, 19, 22, 23, 24.*
a) Which were the remaining 7 tribes still to be given land?
b) How did Moses look ahead to this day?

DAY 3 *Joshua 19:49-51; 21:43-45; Deuteronomy 33:26-29.*
a) What was the name of the city that Joshua was given?
b) List some of the things you can find out about God from these readings.

DAY 4 *Joshua 20:1-9; Deuteronomy 19:1-13.*
a) What was the purpose of the cities of refuge?
b) What were they a picture of (see Prov. 18:10; Ps. 46:1)?

DAY 5 *Joshua 21:1-8; Numbers 35:1-8.*
(Look back to Study 9, Day 4.)
a) Why were the Levites not given an area of land for their own?
b) How many cities throughout the land were they given?

DAY 6 *Joshua 22:1-9.*
(Look back to Study 9, Day 6.)
a) Where was 'home' for the people of Reuben, Gad and the half-tribe of Manasseh?
b) For what did Joshua commend these tribes?

DAY 7 *Joshua 22:10-34.*
Put this part of the story briefly in your own words.

There is tremendous significance in what is happening at this point in the story. The land of Canaan is being divided among the remaining tribes as God, the Supreme Organizer, directs. For each tribe, there is an inheritance ordained by God, a place of blessing and rest. So, to each believer today, the same Lord offers spiritual blessings and rest.

Is this challenge from Joshua relevant to you?

'How long are you going to wait before you go in and take the land that the Lord has given you?'

Are you aware of the rich treasures in Jesus which are available to you when you put out your hand and take them?

In Tanzania, East Africa, there is an area of land covering 25 square miles, which, until the 1940s was inhabited by the local Africans. Then Dr Williamson, a Canadian with expert geological knowledge, visited the area and felt sure that there were diamonds there. For nine months he wandered around looking, until one day he found what he was looking for and what only a trained eye would recognize – an uncut diamond at the base of a tree. Excitedly he made a more detailed examination, signed a contract with the government to buy the land, and pegged out his claim. To compensate the Africans for the loss of their land, a figure was agreed upon and paid and they moved off. Today in those 25 square miles is one of the world's open cut diamond mines, turning out one million dollars' worth of diamonds every month.

But think of those Africans who had lived on that land. They were the richest families in the country but they didn't realize it. When their children played in the dirt, they played with diamonds; when the parents dug the ground and planted corn and millet, they planted them in diamonds; when they built their mud houses they plastered them with diamonds – but they did not know it! They existed, scratching out a living from that soil, without realizing they could have had wealth unlimited!

How are you living? Like a spiritual pauper – or a millionaire?

'How long are you going to wait before you go in and take the land?'

THE CITIES OF REFUGE

Francis Schaeffer, in his book *Joshua and the flow of Biblical History*, sees the cities of refuge as a powerful illustration of the work of Christ. This is borne out by Hebrews 6:18-20, where we read, 'We have fled for refuge to lay hold upon the hope set before us ... Even Jesus.'

The parallels are as follows:

1) The cities were easily accessible to all.
Christ is within the reach of anyone who realizes his need of Him.

2) The cities were open to all; to the Israelite, the stranger and the traveller.
Christ is available to all people without discrimination.

3) From non-Biblical sources we discover that the gates of these cities were never locked.
So Christ never sleeps, or is tired or too busy. Twenty-four hours a day He holds out His hands saying, 'Come unto Me'.

4) The cities not only provided legal protection, but also were stocked with food to meet the needs of those who entered.
Christ is a totally sufficient refuge. He not only makes the believer eternally safe through His atoning death but also supplies his every need.

5) If a killer did not flee to the city of refuge there was no hope for him, he was doomed.
Similarly, those who are outside of Christ are without hope. There is no other refuge from the fearful consequences of sin.

However, here the parallel ends, because the cities were for the protection of the innocent, the man who killed by mistake. But Christ died for the ungodly, the guilty, the deliberate sinner, that he might have a sure refuge and enjoy eternal fellowship with the Lord.

> How firm a foundation, ye saints of the Lord
> Is laid for your faith in His excellent Word
> What more can He say than to you He hath said,
> You who unto Jesus for refuge have fled:
>
> 'Fear not, I am with thee, Oh be not dismayed,
> For I am thy God and will still give thee aid!
> I'll strengthen thee, help thee, and cause thee to stand
> Upheld by My righteous omnipotent hand.
>
> 'The soul that on Jesus hath leaned for repose
> I will not, I will not desert to its foes;
> That soul, though all hell should endeavour to shake,
> I'll never, no, never, no never forsake!'

STUDY 12

PUT GOD FIRST

QUESTIONS

DAY 1 *Joshua 23:1-6.*
a) Whom did Joshua call to this meeting?
b) What advice did he give them? (Compare this with Deut. 32:45-47).

DAY 2 *Joshua 23:6-16.*
a) Joshua says 8 things about the people's relationship with the Lord in these verses. What are they? It will help if you underline the word 'Lord' (or He) in your Bible first.
b) What does this teach us about the character of God?

DAY 3 *Joshua 24:1-13.*
a) What is God saying through Joshua here?
b) Share with your group some time you can look back to and say, 'God was guiding my life then.'

DAY 4 *Joshua 24:14, 15.*
a) As a result of what we read yesterday, what does Joshua challenge the people to do?
b) What 3 kinds of gods were they to choose between?

DAY 5 *Joshua 24:15-24.*
a) What splendid example did Joshua give the people?
b) What choice did they make?
c) What was to be the proof of their decision (see Matt. 7:21)?

DAY 6 *Joshua 24:25-28.*
a) What did Joshua do to help the people remember their promise? Read Acts 17:11 and Hebrews 10:25.
b) What can we do to help us remember our promise to serve God?

DAY 7 *Joshua 24:29-33; Judges 2:6-10.*
a) How long did the people keep their promise to put God first?
b) Joshua's life had been a tremendous influence on the people of Israel. Can you think of someone who has influenced your life toward Jesus Christ?

NOTES

There is a marvellous unity about the Bible from beginning to end, and the same Holy Spirit who inspired the writings of Moses and Joshua also spoke through men like John and Paul.

So we should not be surprised to find that the message of 'Put God First' rings through His Word from Genesis to Revelation with insistent regularity.

Look at these verses:

'You shall have no other gods before me' (Exod. 20:3).
'Get rid of the gods which your ancestors used to worship and serve only the Lord' (Josh. 24:14).
'In everything you do, put God first and he will direct you' (Prov. 3:6).
'You cannot serve God and money' (Matt 6:24).
'Seek first His Kingdom and His righteousness' (Matt. 6:33).
'It is no longer I who live, but it is Christ who lives in me' (Gal. 2:20).
'Set your minds on things that are above, not on things that are on earth' (Col. 3:2).
'Do not love the world ... for if you love the world you do not love the Father' (I John 2:15).

* * *

As Joshua's life drew to a close, He asked the people a question: 'From this moment on, who is going to control your life?'

And the Lord is asking you the same thing now, as this study of the book of Joshua comes to a close. *'From this moment on, who is going to control your life?'*

It is a solemn moment because the question requires an answer.

Consider the 3 possibilities:

1. *The gods your ancestors worshipped.*
Joshua was referring to the time before God called Abraham to be the father of His people. Back in their ancestry was a time when God the Lord was unknown and the people worshipped gods which gratified human instincts and selfish desires.

But this is true for each of us, too. Before you came into a personal relationship with Christ, there was a time when everything you did was to please yourself, not God. 'Self' was in control and how easy it is still to slip back into those ways of putting self first!

2. *The gods of the Amorites, in whose land you are living.*
Remember, the Israelites had not completely obeyed God, they had not driven out all the people of the land. They had not become a separate, holy people, and it was all too easy to be influenced by those around them.

Isn't that still true? 'So what ... everybody's doing it!' 'You've got to keep up with the times.' The world around us tries to squeeze us into its own mould (remember Caleb?) Advertising dictates how we shall spend our money. 'The Joneses' see to it that we keep up our standard of living. Public opinion via the media hands us our values. It is very hard to stand against these and other pressures and not be controlled by them – in fact, there is only one way to do it.

3. *The Lord.*

To serve the Lord is to recognize that He is the Master and I am the servant. Because I belong to Him, my purpose in living is to do what He wants and to be available for Him to use. Each day I must come before Him to find out His plan for me for that particular day and to surrender my will to His. It is not important what I want, or what other people say – the only thing that matters is that His will should be done through my life.

That is what Paul meant when he said,

'You should have as little desire for this world as a dead person.... It is no longer I who live but it is Christ who lives in me.'

No wonder Joshua warned the people to think carefully before they made their choice, for when a person makes the decision to serve the Lord, it means a total commitment of himself, so that God can work in every area of his life to transform him into His likeness.

'Decide today whom you will serve.'

ANSWER GUIDE

The following pages contain an Answer Guide. It is recommended that answers to the questions be attempted before turning to this guide. It is only a guide and the answers given should not be treated as exhaustive.

GUIDE TO INTRODUCTORY STUDY

Leaders should note that the introductory study will have to be carefully prepared beforehand.

Page 5
This is designed to be an icebreaker and to help new people realize that the Bible is relevant to their situations today.
Your own attitude will help enormously.
Encourage people to share experiences and examples relating to the questions.
If you have several new people in your group (and let's hope you have) you may find it easier to find and read the references yourself, to keep discussion flowing.

Page 6
Study the diagram well beforehand to see what it's all about.

Page 7
The truths discussed in this section are fairly deep, but most are important, so this page particularly will need extra-prayerful preparation. The concept of 'resting' in Christ will be brought out a number of times during the studies, so if people don't grasp it at first, pray that they will before the studies finish.
Read Joshua 24:5-13 carefully beforehand.
Divide the verses into 3 sections:

- those about the deliverance from Egypt
- those about the wilderness
- those about Canaan

In this way you will be better able to help your group understand the diagram. (Make sure people know what 'analogy' means).
If you don't have 12 weeks for this study leave out either Study 10, Study 11, or both, but make sure you do Study 12 on your final day.

GUIDE TO STUDY 1

DAY 1
a) Fighting and defeating the Amalekites. Waiting for Moses while he was up Mt. Sinai. Staying in the tent of Worship. Going to spy out the land.
b) In spite of difficulties, he trusted God to give them the land.

DAY 2
a) The Lord God would go before them and Joshua would be their leader.
b) The Lord.
c) Writing God's Law in a book and giving it into the safe keeping of the priests.

DAY 3
a) That He would bring the people into a rich and fertile land.
b) Because Moses was dead and because the Lord told him so.

DAY 4
a) That he would not be defeated; That God would always be with him. Probably weak, fearful and discouraged (remember the great leader Moses had just died) so God spoke to encourage him.
b) We may know through experience or because He says so in His Word.

DAY 5
a) To study and meditate on His Word day and night.
b) Personal.

DAY 6
a) Because God was always with them and never left them alone.
b) What pleased God.
c) Joshua 1:7.

DAY 7
a) Their wives, children and cattle could stay on the east side of Jordan, in the land allotted to them, but they were to fight with the other tribes until they had taken possession of the land.
b) They were willing to obey him and wished him God's blessing.

GUIDE TO STUDY 2

DAY 1 a) He sent two spies to explore Canaan, especially Jericho.
b) She was a prostitute and sympathetic to the Israelite spies.

DAY 2 a) That all the people of Jericho were terrified of the Israelites because they realized their God was more powerful than any other god.
b) She had faith in God, even though she knew very little about Him.

DAY 3 a) Rahab's house was on the city wall and she let them down by a rope from her window.
b) She tied the scarlet cord to the window.

DAY 4 a) 'The Lord has given you the land (or city).' (Note that the verb is in the past tense, though the Living Bible alters this.)
b) Their absolute faith in what God was going to do.

DAY 5 a) Her faith.
b) Her actions.
c) A person is saved through faith, but their faith is shown by their actions.

DAY 6 a) If Rahab's house on the wall would collapse too! (i.e., if God might not save her after all.)
b) To safety beside the Israelite camp.

DAY 7 a) She was an ancestor of David and therefore of Jesus Christ. Her husband's name was Salmon (was he perhaps one of the spies she had hidden?) and her son's name Boaz.
b) She brought joy to the heart of God when she (obviously) gave up her life of sin and became one of God's people.

JOSHUA • ANSWER GUIDE • • • • •

GUIDE TO STUDY 3

DAY 1 a) To follow the ark of the covenant (and to keep a small distance away from it).
Because they had never been there before and the ark would guide them.
b) Because He had been through them Himself and had won the victory.

DAY 2 a) To purify (sanctify) themselves.
Because the next day the Lord would perform miracles among them.
b) Purify ourselves from everything that makes body or soul unclean. (Leaders, get some suggestions from your group as to what kind of things are meant here).

DAY 3 a) The ark of the covenant.
b) Keep our eyes fixed on Jesus.
He is the supreme example of how to live the Christian life; thinking of Him brings encouragement; we remember to submit to Him afresh; He takes our eyes off our problems; etc.

DAY 4 a) The Christian life is lived by trust in God (whom we cannot see), and we must not look at it from the human point of view.
b) By faith in Jesus Christ.

DAY 5 a) That God was right there with them as they passed through the waters (this can also refer to trials and suffering).
b) They were actually to put their feet into the water before God would dry up the river bed.

DAY 6 a) The river was in flood.
b) The Israelites came through by faith, while the Egyptians had no faith in God.

DAY 7 a) Eight times.
It shows its importance in this story.
b) Personal.

GUIDE TO STUDY 4

DAY 1   Tell the priests to walk into the Jordan and stand still. Choose 12 men to take 12 stones from the middle of the Jordan and carry them to where you will camp tonight. Command the priests to come out of the water.

DAY 2   The people. The 12 men chosen, one from each tribe. The priests.

DAY 3   a) All of them.
b) In the middle of the Jordan, where the priests had stood.

DAY 4   a) As a truly great man, they stood in awe of him.
b) He wanted to show the people that He was with Joshua exactly as He had been with Moses.

DAY 5   a) That God dried up the waters of Jordan until His people had crossed over.
b) The Israelites will remember and praise God. Everyone on earth will know how great God's power is.
c) They were terrified.

DAY 6   a) Personal (e.g., they might tell how they crossed the river or be singing praises to God for His great power).
b) God raising Jesus from the dead.

DAY 7   a) God's covenant with His people.
b) They kept the Passover.
c) Exodus 12:26 and Joshua 4:21 both remind us to pass on God's dealings to future generations.

GUIDE TO STUDY 5

DAY 1   a) Possibly to have a good look at it, to see how best to attack.
b) A man with a sword in his hand, the commander of the Lord's army.

DAY 2   a) Supernatural forces and also the people of Israel.
b) He worshipped and asked what he was to do.

DAY 3   a) The people were to march round the city once a day for 6 days and 7 times on the 7th day. On the 7th day the priests were to sound the trumpets and the people to shout after the long blast on the trumpets.
b) From a human point of view, it was a foolish and ineffective thing to do.

DAY 4   a) Perhaps you would laugh at first. You would feel apprehensive as this went on day after day and you would be afraid (see v. 1).
b) See Notes for this study under heading 'THE VICTORY'.

DAY 5   a) It describes each man in the army going straight ahead into the city as the walls had fallen flat.
b) By His Spirit.

DAY 6   a) Superhuman forces of evil. (Different versions give interesting wording of Eph. 6:12.)
b) The sword of the Spirit (The Word of God), prayer, and of course, faith!

DAY 7   a) Because the people were so wicked, their punishment was due.
b) Rahab, her father, mother, brothers and all who belonged to her.
c) The things made of gold, silver, bronze and iron.

Leaders, as you plan this week's study, read the Notes carefully and allow enough time for people to think deeply about the whole principle of the lesson.

   If questions arise about God's orders to destroy all the people, defer this till next week when the subject will be discussed in the Notes.

GUIDE TO STUDY 6

DAY 1
a) That only 2-3,000 men should attack, as it was only a small city. (They were confident in their own strength, not dependant on God's.)
b) They were forced to retreat and 36 men were killed.
c) They were 'paralysed with fear' (Living Bible).

DAY 2
a) They came and talked to the Lord about it.
b) That the Canaanites would feel they were easy prey and kill them. That people would no longer honour God's Name; They might have feared that God would leave them.

DAY 3
a) Israel had sinned and broken God's command.
b) The love of money.

DAY 4
a) A beautiful Babylonian cloak, 200 shekels of silver and a bar of gold weighing 50 shekels.
b) He saw, he coveted, he took and he hid.
c) That He, like His Father, reacted in righteous anger against sin and warned people against eternal judgment.

DAY 5
a) To take all the soldiers, send some into ambush beyond the city, and the others would lure out the men of Ai, leaving the city unprotected.
b) The city and its king were to be destroyed but the Israelites could keep the goods and cattle for themselves. (Achan could have waited!)

DAY 6
a) Personal.
b) They were pursuing the main part of the army and they didn't know about the ambush.

DAY 7
a) He pointed his spear at the city and kept it there until every one of the inhabitants were killed.
b) The men from the ambush came down behind them and the army they were pursuing turned round and fought them.

JOSHUA • ANSWER GUIDE • . . . .

GUIDE TO STUDY 7

DAY 1   a) On Mount Ebal.
b) some large stones covered with plaster.
(N.B. As Mt. Ebal is 30 miles from Gilgal, the stones could not have been taken from the river where they crossed so the Living Bible is incorrect.)
c) Clearly.

DAY 2   a) I. Mt. Ebal. 2. Mt. Gerizim.
b) Six on each.
c) The ark of the covenant.

DAY 3   a) Personal. (e.g. v. 16, v. 19, v. 24, v. 26)
b) 'Amen' means 'so be it', or 'I agree'. This helped the people to identify with and thus remember God's laws.

DAY 4   a) Make a covenant (or treaty) with any of the people of Canaan or let them live among them.
b) They took worn out sacks, patched wineskins, ragged clothes and shoes, and mouldy bread to pretend they lived a long distance away.

DAY 5   a) They didn't bother to ask the Lord (LB) before believing what was said and signing the treaty.
b) Personal (e.g., God warns against marriage between a Christian and an unbeliever, against trying to live the world's way and God's).

DAY 6   a) They were to be slaves, cutting wood and carrying water for God's people and His altar.
b) Because they had given a solemn promise before God that they would not.

DAY 7   a) They were to choose between good and evil, life and death, God's blessing and God's curse.
b) Personal. (e.g., the Bible is God's word revealed to men. Has man the ability to make wise decisions without guidelines? God never changes, etc.)

GUIDE TO STUDY 8

DAY 1 a) He would give him the entire land (a map would be useful here.); No one would be able to defeat him; God would always be with him.
b) Allowing God to work through us.

DAY 2 a) They deceived Joshua and the leaders of Israel into making a treaty with them.
b) They were being surrounded and attacked by the combined forces from 5 cities.
c) 'I have already given you the victory' (v. 8).

DAY 3 V. 10 He made the Amorites panic.
V. 11 He sent large hailstones.
V. 12 He gave Israel the victory.
V. 14 He altered the course of nature at the request of a human being (stopped the sun and moon).
V. 14 He fought on Israel's side.

DAY 4 a) We have enemies to fight – not physical but spiritual. Just as the Lord fought for Joshua and won the victory, so He has already won the victory against Satan for us. We only need to claim the victory.
b) Joshua told them that the Lord would do this to all their enemies.

DAY 5 a) That these victories were entirely the Lord's.
b) That their entrance into the land was entirely due to a miracle by the Lord.

DAY 6 a) Verse 4 'as many men as there are grains of sand on the sea shore' (GNB); 'A vast array ... as far as one could see' (LB).
b) They had horses and chariots.
c) The Lord gave Joshua a special message (v. 6).

DAY 7 a) Obedience to God's commands brings victory.
b) Personal.

GUIDE TO STUDY 9

DAY 1 a) King Sihon would not let them, but he gathered his army together and attacked them. The Israelites killed the people and occupied their land.
King Og marched out and attacked the Israelites as they went towards his territory, so they killed him and his army, and occupied the land.
b) Moses.

DAY 2 a) On the defence (except for Jericho and Ai).
b) 31.

DAY 3 a) There was still much land to be taken.
b) He was to divide up the land among the tribes who were then to possess their own area.
c) Personal.

DAY 4 a) Any part of the land for their own.
b) A share of the sacrificial meat.
Cities (spread over the whole land) to live in, with fields for their cattle and flocks.

DAY 5 a) That He would provide for them with food from the offerings of the people. That He, the Lord, would be their sufficiency (v. 20).
b) That they would have the privilege of being the Lord's priests. (Notice that the N.T. references given are similar to the promises to the Levites.)

DAY 6 South: Reuben; Middle: Gad;
North: half of the tribe of Manasseh.

DAY 7 a) Eleazar the priest, Joshua and the leaders of the tribes divided it by drawing lots as the Lord had commanded Moses.
b) Not to be spiritually lazy or slack, but eager to press forward all the time.

GUIDE TO STUDY 10

DAY 1
a) They first said it was a good land (then denied this in 13:32!) but they said they would never be able to possess it because the people there were very powerful and their cities well fortified.
b) Joshua and Caleb said they could easily conquer the land, because the Lord was with them.
c) He promised to give Caleb the part of the land that he had explored.

DAY 2
a) 'Give me the hill country that the Lord promised me' (v. 12).
b) 1. 40. 2. 85.

DAY 3
a) He faithfully obeyed the Lord.
b) He was different because he trusted God implicitly and was loyal to Him.
c) Personal.

DAY 4
a) He drove out the descendants of Anak and found that the Lord was with him and did give him victory.
b) She asked for land with water in it.

DAY 5
a) Judah, Ephriam and Manasseh (i.e., descendants of Joseph).
b) Caleb drove out the people of the land as the Lord had commanded, whereas the others didn't.

DAY 6
a) Because their father had died without leaving any sons and they wanted his descendants to have a share in the land.
b) The Lord.

DAY 7
a) Because there were too many of them.
b) To clear the hill country of forest and settle there. To drive out the people of the plains even though they had iron chariots.

GUIDE TO STUDY 11

DAY 1   a) 'How long are you going to wait before you go in and take the land?'
b) To go out over all the land and map it out.

DAY 2   a) Benjamin, Simeon, Zebulun, Issachar, Asher, Naphtali and Dan.
b) He prophesied a blessing for every tribe.

DAY 3   a) Timnath Serah
b) The Lord gave them victory and kept every one of His promises He had made. He is unique, magnificent, our defence, protector, shield and sword.

DAY 4   a) A person who killed someone accidentally could go there and escape a relative looking for revenge.
b) The Lord who is our refuge (see also Ps. 46:1).

DAY 5   a) Because they were to remember that the Lord God was all they needed (Num. 18:20).
b) 48.

DAY 6 ·   a) On the east of the river Jordan.
b) They had done everything Moses had told them to do, i.e., they had not deserted their fellow Israelites but had fought with them for their land.

DAY 7   Personal.

GUIDE TO STUDY 12

DAY 1   a) All Israel, the elders, leaders, judges and officers of the people.
b) He told them to be sure they obeyed God's law.

DAY 2   a) V. 8 Be faithful to the Lord.
V. 9 The Lord has driven out your enemies.
V. 10 The Lord is fighting for you as He promised.
V. 11 Love the Lord.
V. 13 If you are disloyal, the Lord will no longer drive out your enemies.
V. 13 The Lord has given you the land.
V. 14 The Lord has kept His promises.
V. 16 If you do not keep the Lord's covenant, He will punish you.
b) He is powerful, and faithful to His promises, but will punish those who forsake Him.

DAY 3   a) That since the days of Abraham, God was in control and guided His people.
b) Personal.

DAY 4   a) Decide today whom you will serve.
b) The gods your ancestors worshipped; the gods of the Amorites, or , The Lord God.

DAY 5   a) He said, 'As for me and my house, we will serve the Lord.'
b) To serve the Lord.
c) Getting rid of their idols and obeying God.

DAY 6   a) He wrote God's rules in a book and also set up a stone of remembrance.
b) Read the Bible every day and worship with other Christians.

DAY 7   a) As long as Joshua lived, and then as long as the leaders of Joshua's day were alive.
b) Personal.

JOSHUA • ANSWER GUIDE

•
•
•
•
•

THE WORD WORLDWIDE

We first heard of WORD WORLDWIDE over 20 years ago when Marie Dinnen, its founder, shared excitedly about the wonderful way ministry to one needy woman had exploded to touch many lives. It was great to see the Word of God being made central in the lives of thousands of men and women, then to witness the life-changing results of them applying the Word to their circumstances. Over the years the vision for WORD WORLDWIDE has not dimmed in the hearts of those who are involved in this ministry. God is still at work through His Word and in today's self-seeking society, the Word is even more relevant to those who desire true meaning and purpose in life. WORD WORLDWIDE is a ministry of WEC International, an interdenominational missionary society, whose sole purpose is to see Christ known, loved and worshipped by all, particularly those who have yet to hear of His wonderful name. This ministry is a vital part of our work and we warmly recommend the WORD WORLDWIDE 'Geared for Growth' Bible studies to you. We know that as you study His Word you will be enriched in your personal walk with Christ. It is our hope that as you are blessed through these studies, you will find opportunities to help others discover a personal relationship with Jesus. As a mission we would encourage you to work with us to make Christ known to the ends of the earth.

Stewart and Jean Moulds – British Directors, **WEC International.**

A full list of over 50 'Geared for Growth' studies can be obtained from:

ENGLAND   *North East/South*: John and Ann Edwards
5 Louvaine Terrace, Hetton-le-Hole, Tyne & Wear, DH5 9PP
Tel. 0191 5262803 Email: rhysjohn.edwards@virgin.net
North West/Midlands: Anne Jenkins
Tel. 01524 734797 Email: anne@jenkins.abelgratis.com
West: Pam Riches Tel. 01594 834241

IRELAND   Steffney Preston
33 Harcourts Hill, Portadown, Craigavon, N. Ireland, BT62 3RE
Tel. 028 3833 7844 Email: sa.preston@talk21.com

SCOTLAND   Margaret Halliday
10 Douglas Drive, Newton Mearns, Glasgow, G77 6HR
Tel. 0141 639 8695 Email: mhalliday@onetel.net.uk

WALES   William and Eirian Edwards
Penlan Uchaf, Carmarthen Road, Kidwelly, Carms., SA17 5AF
Tel. 01554 890423 Email: penlanuchaf@fwi.co.uk

UK CO-ORDINATOR
Anne Jenkins
2 Windermere Road, Carnforth, Lancs., LA5 9AR
Tel. 01524 734797 Email: anne@jenkins.abelgratis.com

UK Website: www.wordworldwide.org.uk

JOSHUA